Mailbox Ministry

Mailbox Ministry

Greeting Cards that Share the Faith

Sue Banker

Morehouse Publishing

An imprint of Church Publishing Incorporated

HARRISBURG—NEW YORK

Morehouse Publishing, 4775 Linglestown Road, Harrisburg, PA 17112

Morehouse Publishing, 445 Fifth Avenue, New York, NY 10016

Morehouse Publishing is an imprint of Church Publishing Incorporated.

Cover and card art by Sue Banker
Cover and interior photography by Andy Lyons Cameraworks
Cover design by Brenda Klinger
Interior design by Beth Oberholtzer

ISBN: 978-0-8192-2307-4

Library of Congress Cataloging-in-Publication Data
A catalog record of this book is available from the Library of Congress.

Printed in Malaysia
09 10 11 12 13 14   10 9 8 7 6 5 4 3 2 1

for my grandparents, Lilah and Elmer Liljander, who instilled
in me a deep appreciation for creations made by hand

for my parents, Sally and Richard Aker, who encouraged me
to grow in my faith and pursue my passion for art and writing

for my brothers, Scott and Mark Aker, who taught me
the significance of humor, modesty, and perseverance

for my husband, Richard Banker, who affectionately offers
his kind words of wisdom and unending support

for my children, Ryan and Morgan, who share their honest opinions,
unconditional love, and world's best hugs

for my many friends who continuously strengthen my faith
in God and remind me of the many blessings of friendship

for crafters, writers, communicators, and fellow believers everywhere

may they be showered with abundant blessings
as they too share God's love

CONTENTS

love one another

INTRODUCTION

For this is the message you have heard from the beginning,
that we should love one another.

—1 JOHN 3:11

Encouraged by the Apostle Paul's letters preaching that we should love
one another, devoted Christians around the world graciously offer acts of
kindness. We share our time, talent, and treasure with others, and we do our
best to provide a helping hand to those in need. Sometimes, though, it is difficult to know how to reach out to those around us, how to communicate our
happiness for others' good fortune, or our concern for their troubles. At times,
we may want to just let someone know that we are there, that we care about
what is going on in his or her life, that we remember a milestone or notice a
job well done.

In bad times, words of support help comfort the soul. Throughout our lives
here on earth we will have to face adversities, such as the loss of a job, illness,

OPPOSITE: *Love One Another; instructions, pages 70–71.*

and death of a loved one. When we feel the concern and prayers of others, it lifts the spirit and helps us cope with even the most difficult of situations.

I often think back on the year when I lost my mom and brother within four months of each other. Being the last one in our immediate family, I suffered with grief. Later that year the Twin Towers were struck down in New York City. I was so saddened by the year's events that I often felt paralyzed. As I prayed for help and understanding, my mailbox kept filling with empathy. Sincerely-written cards and letters flooded in from friends, family, and fellow church members. Looking back, I'm not sure how I would, or could, have made it through such an unbearable time without their acts of kindness. It was the compassion of others that held me up and made me strong enough to move on.

In good times, receiving congratulatory greetings from others amplifies the joy. Whether it's a birth, birthday, anniversary, or holiday, we are honored when others share in our happiness. I feel extremely blessed that I have a wonderful network of friends and extended family that remember me on every cheerful occasion with cards brimming with good wishes.

One way we creatively show our caring for one another is by the giving of greeting cards. Using cards as a vehicle of communication, we can spread God's love in a beautiful, meaningful, and memorable manner. The words and creative presentations we share through greeting cards can be quite significant, even life altering and profound.

No matter what the tone of occasion— sad, happy, or just because—handmade greeting cards show sincere thoughtfulness and enable you to personalize each message. *Mailbox Ministry: Greeting Cards that Share the Faith* offers dozens of ideas for faith-filled cards you can make, blanket with prayer, and give with love. You'll also find card-making tips throughout the book, including inspirational messages to write and ideas for building a card ministry within your church.

I hope you find the pages that follow to be filled with inspiration for your own greeting card ministry. Most of all, I pray you feel God's divine love as you touch the lives of others with these small, tangible signs of your thoughtfulness.

CHAPTER ONE

IN NEED OF PRAYERS

When the cares of my heart are many,
your consolations cheer my soul.

—PSALMS 94:19

When I was eleven years old, I had an accident that kept me home from school for nearly a month. I was ice skating at our local outdoor rink and decided to go in the warming shack to rest and thaw my snow-covered mittens. When I pulled on the shack door, the pulley-and-weight system was so heavy it whipped me against the door frame, hitting my cheek against the lock. By the time I walked the two blocks home, my eye was swollen shut and it looked as though half a baseball was in its place. After a trip to the doctor and a painful outpatient procedure, I was sent home to rest—for weeks—in a darkened room. No language or art classes. No ringing handbells at church. No hopscotch or jump rope. Nothing but rest.

OPPOSITE: *Matted Cross; instructions, pages 3–4.*
Rays of Light; instructions, pages 5–6.

As a busy, social, school-loving fifth grader, I didn't like being home while my friends were at school. I also tired of lying in a dark room with limited television time due to the strain on my good eye. I was sore, lonely, and bored.

From those weeks though, there are a few joyous memories I cherish. One is of Grandma serving me her famous fried egg sandwiches on a t.v. tray. Another is of my friends stopping to visit me on their way home from school. They made a game out of hiding little objects in my blanket that I would try to find just by feeling for them.

Yet another blessing is the memory of the day the mailman delivered an oversized envelope right to our door. It was the first mail I remember receiving that was addressed directly to me. The big yellow clasp envelope was stuffed with handmade cards, one from each of my classmates. Those cards helped me feel a special connection to my school, teacher, and friends, and reminded me that others were thinking of me during my recovery.

That is the intention of the cards in this chapter. While you can customize them to send whatever message is needed, I pray they help you reach out to people in times of upset, sadness, and worry with God's promise that we are never alone.

Matted Cross

As shown on page xii.

Worn-look papers handsomely frame a center cross motif, reminding us that Jesus is our Savior.

> Folded card size: 6 inches square
>
> Envelope size: 6^1/$_2$ inches square

Supplies

> ruler
>
> pencil
>
> scoring tool
>
> 6x12-inch piece of patterned paper
>
> 3^1/$_2$ -inch square of tan suede paper
>
> 3-inch square of light blue paper
>
> 2^1/$_2$ -inch square of bright blue paper
>
> 1^3/$_4$ -inch circle of dull silver paper
>
> 5^3/$_4$ x11^1/$_2$ -inch piece of liner paper
>
> circle maker to cut 2-, 2^1/$_4$ -, and 2^3/$_4$ -inch diameters
>
> 1^1/$_2$ -inch high cross punch
>
> glue stick

Make the Card

1. Measure and mark the center of each long edge of the 6x12-inch piece of patterned paper. Score the card center using the marks as a guide. Fold the paper in half along scored line.

2. Using a circle maker, cut a 2^3/$_4$ -inch-diameter circle in the center of the card front. Cut a 2^1/$_4$ -inch-diameter circle in the center of the tan suede paper.

*To you, O Lord,
I lift up my soul.
O my God,
in you I trust.*

Psalms 25:1—2

3. Use the cross punch to cut out a cross shape in the center of the bright blue paper. Cut a $2^1/4$ -inch-diameter circle around the cross shape.

4. Adhere the light blue paper centered behind the suede paper, allowing it to show through circle cut in card front.

5. Adhere the silver paper behind the cross shape; glue to center of card.

6. Measure and mark the center of each long edge of the $5^3/4$ x$11^1/2$ liner paper. Score the liner using the marks as a guide. Fold the paper in half along scored line and glue to inside of card.

Inside Inspirations

Rejoice with those who rejoice, weep with those who weep. —Rom. 12:15

We are so very sorry for your loss.

Give rest, O Christ, to thy servant with thy saints, where sorrow and pain are no more, neither sighing, but life everlasting. —Book of Common Prayer, 482

Please know that you are in our thoughts and prayers, and we are eager to help in any way we can.

TIP: **While this card is 6 inches square, you can make it as small as $3^1/2$ inches square using the same circle dimensions.**

Do not withhold good from those to whom it is due, when it is in your power to do it.

Proverbs 3:27

Rays of Light

As shown on page xii.

Help heal the spirit with cheerful get-well wishes.

Folded card size: $4^{1}/_{4}$ x$5^{1}/_{2}$ inches

Envelope size: $4^{3}/_{8}$ x$5^{3}/_{4}$ inches

Supplies

ruler

pencil

scoring tool

$5^{1}/_{2}$ x8-inch piece of cardstock

three $5^{1}/_{2}$ -inch-long pieces of ribbon

$3^{1}/_{2}$ -inch-long piece of ribbon

glue stick

button(s)

embroidery floss

sewing needle

vellum sentiment

sticker or embroidered appliqué

double-stick tape

Make the Card

1. Measure and mark $3^{3}/_{4}$ inches from one short edge of the cardstock. Score the card using the marks as a guide. Fold the paper in along scored line.

2. Use glue stick to adhere the three $5^{1}/_{2}$ -inch-long pieces of ribbon to the bottom of the card front as desired.

*Protect me,
O God,
for in you
I take refuge.*

Psalms 16:1

3. Align the ends of the short length of ribbon; glue ends together. Thread the needle with embroidery floss. Aligning the loop with the card bottom, sew the ribbon loop and button(s) to the center of the card flap.

4. Arrange the vellum sentiment and sticker or appliqué on the card. Use double-stick tape to affix the vellum and appliqué in place.

Inside Inspirations

Thinking of you every day.

O merciful Father, who hast taught us in thy holy Word that thou dost not willingly afflict or grieve the children of men: Look with pity upon the sorrows of thy servant for whom our prayers are offered. Remember him/her, O Lord, in mercy, nourish his/her soul with patience, comfort him/her with a sense of thy goodness, lift up thy countenance upon him/her, and give him/her peace; through Jesus Christ our Lord. Amen.
—Book of Common Prayer, 831

We are praying for you.

TIP: **If the vellum needs to lay beneath the button, cut a slit to where the button overlaps and slip the vellum into place.**

Sanctuary Symbols

As shown on page 8.

Pretty papers mimic the glorious views inspired by colorful church windows.

Folded card size: $4^3/4$ x8 inches (arched), $5^1/2$ x8 inches (rectangular)

Envelope size: 6x$8^1/4$

Supplies for All Cards

ruler

pencil

scoring tool

tracing paper

scissors

8x11-inch piece of black cardstock

glue stick

Additional Supplies for Arch Stained Glass Card

scraps of tone-on-tone subtle patterned papers in pink, green, purple, and blue

Additional Supplies for Arch Cross Card

$4^1/2$ x8-inch piece of blue paper

$4^1/2$ x8-inch piece of dull metallic gold paper

$4^1/2$ x8-inch piece of black paper

scraps of paper in purple, pink, red, blue, and orange

paper trimmer

Additional Supplies for Rectangular Cross Card

$4^1/2$ x$7^3/4$ -inch piece of yellow and metallic gold print paper

scraps of paper in gold, bronze, and silver

paper trimmer

Sanctuary Symbols; instructions, pages 7 and 9.

Make the Cards

1. For all cards, measure and mark the center of each long edge of the 8x11-inch piece of black cardstock. Score the card center using the marks as a guide. Fold the paper in half along scored line.

2. For the arch cards, trace the pattern pieces on pages 100–104. Set all patterns, except for the arch pattern, aside. Trace around the arch pattern on the folded card, aligning the left edge of the pattern with the fold. Trim along drawn line.

3. For the arch stained glass card, trace around the window patterns on tone-on-tone papers, mirroring the colors as shown. Cut out the shapes. Glue the pieces to the card front allowing approximately 1/8 inch between pieces.

4. For the arch cross card, use the patterns to cut the blue background shape, gold and black cross shapes, and the gold beams. To make the colored strips on the cross, cut 1/2-inch-long strips from the various colors of paper. Cut the strips into short segments. Glue the blue background and gold beams to the card front. Layer and glue the solid cross shapes to the center of the card. Arrange and glue the colored strips to the center of the cross.

5. For the rectangular cross card, glue the yellow and metallic gold print paper to the card front, leaving equal borders on the top, bottom, and right side. Use the cross pattern to cut the shape from black paper and glue it to the center of the print paper. Cut 1/2-inch-wide strips from metallic papers. Cut the strips into short segments. Arrange and glue the metallic strips to the center of the cross and along the wide black border.

TIP: **To make a quick card, cut a patterned paper using the arch shape and apply it to the rectangular background.**

Bear one another's burdens, and in this way you will fulfill the law of Christ.

GALATIANS 6:2

Prayerfully Yours

As shown on page 11.

Focused on prayers, this card includes gold papers, braid, and letters that bring out the luster of an embossed rosary card.

Folded card size: $5^1/_4$ x8 inches

Envelope size: $5^1/_2$ x$8^1/_8$ inches

Supplies

ruler

pencil

scoring tool

8x$10^1/_2$ -inch piece of metallic gold cardstock

8x5-inch piece of embossed ivory paper

3x4-inch piece of dull metallic gold paper

decorative-edge scissors

glue stick

8-inch length of gold braid

hot-glue gun and hot-melt adhesive

2x$3^1/_4$ -inch rosary card

adhesive foam spacers

metallic gold alphabet stickers

Make the Card

1. Measure and mark the center of each long edge of the 8x$10^1/_2$ -inch piece of cardstock. Score the card center using the marks as a guide. Fold the paper in half along scored line.

The Lord is my rock,
my fortress,
and my deliverer,
my God, my rock in
whom I take refuge,
my shield, and the
horn of my salvation,
my stronghold.

Psalms 18:2

Prayerfully Yours; instructions, pages 10 and 12.
Good Reading; instructions, pages 13–14.

2. Trim off the edges of the ivory and dull gold papers using decorative-edge scissors.

3. Glue the ivory paper to the center of the card front. Position the dull gold paper $3/4$ inch in from the right edge of the card and $1^1/2$ inches up from the bottom.

4. Hot-glue the braid 1 inch in from card fold.

5. Use spacers to adhere the rosary card to the dull gold paper.

6. Place alphabet stickers below rosary card.

Inside Inspirations

> In the Name of the Father and of the Son and of the Holy Ghost,
> we pray for your healing.

> We've been thinking of you.

Good Reading

As shown on page 11.

Give the best gift there is, the words of the New Testament, in an easy-to-take-anywhere size.

Folded card size: 6 inches square

Envelope size: 6^1/$_2$ inches square

Supplies

ruler

pencil

scoring tool

6x12-inch piece of plaid paper

6x12-inch piece of white cardstock

6x1^1/$_2$ -inch piece of coordinating print paper

6x1/$_4$ -inch piece of coordinating paper

glue stick

small New Testament Bible

long-reach paper punch

jute

Make the Card

1. Measure and mark the center of each long edge of the 6x12-inch pieces of plaid paper and cardstock. Score the card centers using the marks as guides. Fold the papers in half along scored lines.

2. Use glue stick to adhere the plaid paper to the cardstock liner.

In my distress I called upon the Lord; to my God I cried for help. From his temple he heard my voice, and my cry to him reached his ears.

PSALMS 18:6

3. Glue the 1½ -inch-wide paper strip ¼ inch from the card fold with the ¼-inch-wide strip next to it.

4. Position the Bible in the framed area on the card front. Use a pencil to mark string holes, measuring 1 inch in each direction from the book corners as shown. Punch out holes as marked using a long-reach paper punch. Thread the jute through the holes, insert the Bible, and tie the ends to secure.

TIP: **Print out a favorite scripture the same size as the Bible. Glue it to the card beneath the Bible for an unexpected message to be revealed when the Bible is removed.**

Inside Inspirations

Blessed are the pure in heart, for they will see God. Matt. 5:8

May the good book always guide your path.

Glorious and Bright

As shown on page 16.

Colorful alphabet stickers set the stage for a vividly clear message.
  Folded card sizes: $3^1/2$ x5 inches (God), $3^1/2$ x$6^1/4$ inches (Peace),
    $4^3/8$ x$7^1/2$ inches (Jesus)

  Envelope sizes: $3^5/8$ x$5^1/8$ inches, $4^3/4$ x$6^1/2$ inches, $5^1/4$ x$7^3/4$ inches

Supplies

  ruler

  pencil

  scoring tool

  white cardstock

  cardstock in desired color and size

  paper in black and/or colors to coordinate with letters

  paper trimmer

  1-inch-high colorful alphabet stickers

  $3/4$-inch square maker

  glue stick

Make the Card

1. Measure and mark the center of cardstock where fold is desired. Score the card center using the marks as a guide. Fold the paper in half along scored line.

2. Arrange sticker letters on white cardstock and trim leaving a narrow border.

Glorious and Bright; instructions, pages 15 and 17.

3. Using the photo for inspiration, mat the word simply or embellish around the word with 3/4-inch paper squares set straight or on point.

Inside Inspirations

Have faith.

For God so loved the world that he gave his only Son, so that everyone who believes in him may not perish but may have eternal life.
—John 3:16

Stamped with Love

As shown on page 20.

A rubber stamp motif that leaves open spaces for colored pencils makes a glorious statement.

Folded card size: 4^{1}/$_{4}$ x6^{1}/$_{2}$ inches

Envelope size: 5^{1}/$_{4}$ x7^{1}/$_{4}$ inches

Supplies

ruler

pencil

scoring tool

6^{1}/$_{2}$ x8^{1}/$_{2}$ -inch piece of watercolor-look paper

cardstock in white and color to coordinate with background

stamp with open areas to color

black stamp pad

colored pencils

glue stick

Be strong, and let your
heart take courage,
all you who wait
for the Lord.

PSALMS 31:24

Hear my prayer, O Lord; let my cry come to you. Do not hide your face from me in the day of my distress. Incline your ear to me; answer me speedily in the day when I call.

PSALMS 102:1–2

Make the Card

1. Measure and mark the center of each long edge of the $6^1/2$ x$8^1/2$ -inch piece of watercolor-look paper. Score the card center using the marks as a guide. Fold the paper in half along scored line.

2. Stamp the image on white cardstock and let dry.

3. Use colored pencils to color in the desired areas of the stamped image. Trim the sides uneven to the stamp. Trim the colored cardstock the same size.

4. Angle and glue the colored cardstock behind the stamping. Glue the papers to the center of the card front.

Inside Inspirations

Whatever we can do. . . we will.

Defend us, deliver us, and in thy compassion protect us, O Lord, by thy grace. —Book of Common Prayer, 385

Hold tight to your faith, knowing that God will hold you up.

TIP: **Stamp paper strips to make bookmarks.**

TIP: **Let children in Sunday school help color in stamped images.**

Thoughtful Stitches

As shown on page 20.

Remember someone with a card elegantly trimmed with simple embroidery stitches.

Folded card size: 4x5$^1/_2$ inches

Envelope size: 4$^3/_8$ x5$^3/_4$ inches

Supplies

ruler

pencil

scoring tool

5$^1/_2$ x8- and 3$^1/_2$ x1-inch pieces of white cardstock

4$^1/_2$ x4- and 4x1$^1/_2$ -inch pieces of patterned paper

4$^1/_8$ x4-inch piece of coordinating paper

glue stick

tracing paper

plastic foam block

large safety pin

sewing needle

embroidery floss in two shades of two colors to coordinate with papers (four colors total)

Make the Card

1. Measure and mark the center of each long edge of the 5$^1/_2$ x8-inch piece of paper. Score the card center using the marks as a guide. Fold the paper in half along scored line.

Stamped with Love; instructions, pages 17–18.
Thoughtful Stitches; instructions, pages 19 and 21.

2. Glue the 4½ x4-inch piece of patterned paper aligned with the left edge of the card. Center and adhere the 4⅛ x4-inch piece of coordinating paper to the rectangle. Glue the 4x1½ -inch piece of paper to the card front, aligned with the right edge, ½ inch from the bottom edge.

3. Trace the desired pattern, page 105. Place the 3½ -inch cardstock strip on the foam block. Place the pattern on top of the cardstock strip, aligning the edges. Use the safety pin to poke the holes as indicated. Remove pattern.

4. For the word, thread the needle with two strands of floss, one of each shade. Knot one end of the floss. Stitch the design using the holes as guides. Switch floss colors to stitch the outline.

5. Glue the stitched rectangle to the 4½-inch paper strip.

Inside Inspirations

Stitched with love, filled with prayers.

May you feel the presence of God, and know that we, your church family, are here to support and help you in any way we can.

TIP: **To stitch other words, print out patterns from a computer using simple, generously spaced fonts.**

Hear my prayer, O Lord; let my cry come to you. Do not hide your face from me in the day of my distress. Incline your ear to me; answer me speedily in the day when I call.

PSALMS 102:1–2

CHAPTER TWO
MOMENTS OF JOY

For you, O Lord, have made me glad by your work;
at the works of your hands I sing for joy.

—PSALMS 92:4

Throughout the year we sprinkle our calendars with reminders regarding the special people in our lives. We jot down birthdays and anniversaries. We record the specifics when babies are born. We take note of holidays, such as Christmas and Easter. In celebration of these joys, we send greeting cards in honor of the occasion.

My husband and children often show their love and respect for me by the presentation of cards. Whether they feature typeset poetry or crayon drawings, each creation touches my heart and reminds me of how thankful I am to be a wife and mom.

When my husband and I started dating, he began the tradition of giving me not just a single card, but several cards in honor of each special occasion.

OPPOSITE: *Gifts from Above; instructions, pages 24–26.*
Wee-One Welcome, instructions, pages 27–28.

The cards are always gorgeous selections, but it's the way he signs the cards that touches me the most. This thought holds true for the cards you'll create. The personal messages your cards deliver will make them uniquely meaningful.

And the handmade cards from my kids are all keepers. Even when they are made with ripped paper or have words misspelled, these from-the-heart cards are irreplaceable treasures with which store-bought cards just can't compete.

The cards in this chapter were created to help celebrate life's happiest moments with cheery handcrafted designs bursting with feel-good wishes. Whether rejoicing the birth of a baby or a Christian holiday, these cards sing with blessings from above.

Gifts from Above
As shown on page 22.

Inspired by tiny baby bracelets, letter beads and charms combine to craft heavenly cards.

Folded card size: $4^{1}/_{2}$ x$5^{7}/_{8}$ inches

Envelope size: $4^{5}/_{8}$ x$6^{1}/_{4}$ inches

Supplies
ruler
pencil
scoring tool
$5^{7}/_{8}$ x9-inch piece of white cardstock
5x$3^{3}/_{4}$ -inch piece of patterned paper for outer background
$4^{3}/_{4}$ x$3^{1}/_{4}$ -inch piece of patterned paper for inner background

glue stick

craft wire

wire cutter

round-tip pliers

large seed beads

small solid or patterned beads

white alphabet beads with black lettering

silver charm

1/8 -inch-wide satin ribbon

scissors

small round adhesive foam spacer

hot-glue gun and hot-melt adhesive

Make the Card

1. Measure and mark the center of each long edge of the 5⅞ x9-inch piece of cardstock. Score the card center using the marks as a guide. Fold the paper in half along scored line.

2. Layer and glue the background rectangles centered on the card front.

3. Use wire cutters to cut a 6-inch piece of wire. To secure beads, curl one wire end using round-tip pliers.

4. Thread three beads onto the wire followed by the desired alphabet beads spaced apart with single seed beads. Thread three more beads onto the wire end, mirroring the bead pattern on the opposite end. Trim the wire to 1/2 inch and curl with round-tip pliers. Shape the wire into a slight curve. Attach a charm between the last two letter beads using a short piece of wire.

You show me the path of life. In your presence there is fullness of joy; in your right hand are pleasures forevermore.

Psalms 16:11

5. Place a foam spacer on the back of each letter and the charm. Adhere to the card front.

6. Use two plies of ribbon to tie a pair of small bows. Hot-glue bows to wire ends.

Inside Inspirations

Our blessings to you and your new gift from heaven.

When a woman is in labor, she has pain, because her hour has come. But when her child is born, she no longer remembers the anguish because of the joy of having brought a human being into the world. —John 16:21

Almighty God, heavenly Father, you have blessed us with the joy and care of children: Give us calm strength and patient wisdom as we bring them up, that we may teach them to love whatever is just and true and good, following the example of our Savior Jesus Christ. Amen. —Book of Common Prayer, 829

You have turned my mourning into dancing; you have taken off my sackcloth and clothed me with joy, so that my soul may praise you and not be silent. O Lord my God, I will give thanks to you forever.

PSALMS 30:11–12

Wee-One Welcome

As shown on page 22.

Send lighthearted greetings filled with oodles of love.

Folded card size: 4⅝ x6 inches

Envelope size: 4¾ x6½ inches

Supplies

ruler

pencil

scoring tool

6x9¼ -inch piece of patterned cardstock

4x5-inch piece of coordinating patterned paper for background

4x4½ -inch piece of coordinating patterned paper

tracing paper

scissors

black fine-tip pen

ivory embroidery floss

hot-glue gun and hot-melt adhesive

2 mini clothespins

Make the Card

1. Measure and mark the center of each long edge of the 6x9¼ -inch piece of cardstock. Score the card center using the marks as a guide. Fold the paper in half along scored line.

2. Glue the background rectangle centered on the card front.

3. Trace the T-shirt pattern on page 105. Use the pattern to cut the desired shape from the remaining patterned paper.

4. Pen stitching lines around the cutouts and background rectangles. Let ink dry.

5. Glue the T-shirt to the center of the card front.

6. Cut an 8-inch piece of embroidery floss. Centering it on the card, hot-glue it in place to the T-shirt shoulders. Knot the floss ends where they meet the top corners of the background paper. Glue knots at corners. Trim floss ends.

7. Hot-glue mini clothespins where the embroidery floss is glued to the clothing item.

Inside Inspirations

God bless the new member of the family!

Jesus loves the little children . . . and so do we! Can't wait to welcome your precious baby into our church family.

TIP: **Simplify the design by deleting the clothesline and pins.**

TIP: **For the diaper motif, replace the clothespin with tiny safety pins poked through the paper.**

Cute as a Button

As shown on page 30.

Pretty polka-dot paper carries through the button theme of this endearing baby card.

Folded card size: 5^1/$_2$ x7^3/$_4$ inches

Envelope size: 6x8^1/$_4$ inches

Supplies

ruler

pencil

scoring tool

7^3/$_4$ x11-inch piece of pink cardstock

7^3/$_4$ x5^1/$_4$ -inch piece of polka-dot paper

7^3/$_4$ x1^3/$_4$ -inch piece of white cardstock

7^3/$_4$ x1^3/$_4$ -inch piece of green paper

3-inch square of pink cardstock

2-inch diameter circle punch

1^1/$_2$ -inch-diameter wood button

decorative-edge scissors

glue stick

10-inch piece of ^{1}/$_8$ -inch-wide pink satin ribbon

hot-glue gun and hot-melt adhesive

small buttons to coordinate with polka-dot paper

alphabet stickers to coordinate with paper colors

But let all who take refuge in you rejoice; let them ever sing for joy. Spread your protection over them, so that those who love your name may exult in you.

PSALMS 5:11

Cute as a Button; instructions, pages 29 and 31.

Make the Card

1. Measure and mark the center of each long edge of the $7^3/4$ x11-inch piece of pink cardstock. Score the card center using the marks as a guide. Fold the paper in half along scored line.

2. Glue the polka-dot rectangle to the card front, centering top to bottom.

3. Trim the edge of the green paper rectangle using decorative-edge scissors. Glue the green strip to the white rectangle, centering top to bottom. Adhere the strip to the card front, approximately $3/4$ inch from the bottom edge.

4. Thread the ribbon through the wood button holes and tie the ends into a bow. Trim the ribbon ends if needed.

5. Cut out a 2-inch circle from the 3-inch square of pink paper. Hot-glue the button on the pink paper circle. Use glue stick to adhere the paper circle to the green paper strip, positioning it $3/8$ inch from the right edge.

6. Use the alphabet stickers to spell out, "cute as a" across the green paper strip.

7. Hot-glue small buttons across the bottom of the card, matching the colors of the polka dots.

Inside Inspirations

Precious as gold. Congratulations!

Watch over thy child, O Lord, as his/her days increase; bless and guide him/her wherever he/she may be. Strengthen him/her when he/she stands; comfort him/her when discouraged or sorrowful; raise him/her up if he/she falls; and in his/her heart may thy peace which passeth understanding abide all the days of his/her life; through Jesus Christ our Lord. Amen.—Book of Common Prayer, 830

I have no greater joy than this, to hear that my children are walking in the truth. —3 John 1:4

Sweet Thoughts

As shown on page 33.

Dimensional or flat, these cupcake cards rise up to honor birthday boys and girls of any age.

Folded card size: 5x7$^{1}/_{2}$ inches

Envelope size: 5$^{1}/_{4}$ x7$^{3}/_{4}$ inches

Supplies

tracing paper

pencil

scissors

7$^{1}/_{2}$ x10-inch piece of solid color or patterned cardstock

4$^{1}/_{8}$ x6$^{5}/_{8}$ -inch piece of solid color embossed cardstock

7x4$^{3}/_{8}$ -inch piece of white paper or 4$^{3}/_{4}$ x7$^{1}/_{4}$ -inch piece of patterned paper

solid papers in two shades of green, dark pink, silver, and either light yellow or light pink

patterned paper for frosting

ruler

scoring tool

candle or scraps of striped and yellow papers and fine-tip black pen

paper trimmer

1-inch-diameter circle punch

pinking shears

glue stick

ribbon, hot-glue gun and hot-melt adhesive, optional

Sweet Thoughts; instructions, pages 32 and 34–35.

Make the Card

1. For either card, trace the cupcake patterns, page 106. Use the patterns to cut shapes from colored and patterned papers. Cut the top edge of the cupcake holder using pinking shears. Set aside the shapes.

2. Measure and mark the center of each long edge of the $7^1/2$ x10-inch piece of patterned cardstock. Score the card center using the marks as a guide. Fold the cardstock in half along scored line.

3. Adhere the paper rectangles to the card front using a glue stick. Adhere the frosting to the cupcake without putting glue on the drips. Place the cupcake bottom behind the holder, arranging the drips on top. Use glue stick to adhere pieces in place. Glue the cupcake centered on the card front, approximately $3/8$ inch from the edge of the inner mat.

4. If desired, use a scoring tool and a ruler to make grooves on the cupcake holder as shown on pattern.

5. Use a circle punch to craft a cherry from dark pink paper. Place glue stick in the center only of the cherry and adhere it to the top of the cupcake. Score a center vein on each leaf if desired. Overlap and glue the leaves on the left side of the cherry.

6. Glue a candle atop the cherry. If using a real candle, run a short line of hot glue on the card front and press the candle into the glue until set. Tie a small ribbon bow and trim the ends. Hot-glue the bow to the base of the candle. (Note: If using a real candle, it is best to hand deliver this card or place it into a well-cushioned envelope.)

Inside Inspirations

May God grant you a blessed birthday that is nothing less than sweet.

Praying your day is filled with many sweet surprises.

TIP: *To make a checkerboard border, such as on the card with the real candle and ribbon, use strips of striped paper. Miter the strips at the corners, enabling the stripes to run both directions.*

Dainty Doilies

As shown on page 37.

Scalloped doilies are so ornate in themselves, it takes but a few moments to turn them into anniversary cards that will be treasured a lifetime.

Folded card size: 6 inches square

Envelope size: 6$1/2$ inches square

Supplies for the 25th Card

ruler

pencil

scoring tool

12-inch square of black-and-white cardstock

5x6-inch piece of bright pink paper

4$1/2$-inch-diameter circle maker

4-inch diameter silver-embossed white doily

tracing paper

decorative-edge scissors

silver dimensional numeral stickers

adhesive foam spacers

Supplies for the 40th Card

ruler

pencil

scoring tool

12-inch square of embossed silver cardstock

5x7-inch piece of bright pink paper

5-inch square of black paper

circle makers in $4^1/4$ -, 2-, and $1^1/2$ -inch diameters

decorative-edge scissors

4-inch white lacy doily

silver dimensional numeral stickers

Make the 25th Card

1. Cut the black-and-white cardstock in half. Measure and mark the center of each long edge. Score the card center using the marks as a guide. Fold the paper in half along scored line.

2. Use the circle maker to cut a $4^1/2$ -inch-diameter circle from pink paper; glue to center of card front. Glue the doily to the center of the pink circle.

3. Trace the heart pattern on page 107. Use the pattern to cut a heart shape from pink paper. Glue heart shape to the leftover black-and-white cardstock and trim a narrow border using decorative-edge scissors. Use foam spacers to adhere the heart to the lower right portion of the doily.

4. Press numeral stickers in the center of the card.

Dainty Doilies; instructions, pages 35–36 and 38.

Make the 40th Card

1. Cut the silver cardstock in half. Measure and mark the center of each long edge. Score the card center using the marks as a guide. Fold the paper in half along scored line.

2. Use the circle maker to cut a $4^{1}/_{4}$ -inch-diameter circle from black paper. Glue the black circle to pink paper and trim a narrow border using decorative-edge scissors. Glue the doily to the center of the black circle. Cut a 2-inch circle from silver paper; glue to doily center. Cut a $1^{1}/_{2}$ -inch-diameter circle from pink paper; glue to center of silver circle.

3. Press numeral stickers in the center of the card.

Inside Inspirations

Congratulations—you two make a heavenly pair!

Make their life together a sign of Christ's love to this sinful and broken world, that unity may overcome estrangement, forgiveness heal guilt, and joy conquer despair. Amen.—Book of Common Prayer, 429

God blessed you (insert number) years ago when you said your "I dos." May He continue to shower your marriage with His love and care each and every day.

Seasonal Salutation

As shown on page 40.

Whether used for a short holiday note or as an invitation, these little beauties sparkle with holiday magic.

Folded card size: 4x4$3/4$ inches

Envelope size: 4$1/8$ x5$1/2$ inches

Supplies for All Cards

ruler

pencil

scoring tool

4$3/4$ x7$1/2$ -inch piece of patterned cardstock

4$3/4$ x1$1/2$ -inch strip of coordinating solid paper

4$3/4$ x1$1/4$ -inch strip of coordinating solid paper

glue stick

1$1/2$ -inch-diameter silver circle stickers

dimensional holiday sticker

gem alphabet stickers

Make the Cards

1. Measure and mark 3$3/4$ inches from one end of the 4$3/4$ x7$1/2$ -inch piece of cardstock. Score the card using the marks as a guide. Fold the paper in along scored line, allowing the front of the card to be shorter than the back.

2. Layer and glue the paper strips to the card front, $1/8$ inch from the bottom edge.

Light dawns for the righteous, and joy for the upright in heart.

PSALMS 97:11

Seasonal Salutation; instructions, pages 39 and 41.
Musical Rendition; instructions, pages 42–43.

3. Press a circle sticker to the paper strips, approximately 3/8 inch from the left edge. Place a dimensional holiday sticker in the circle.

4. Use the gem alphabet stickers to spell out the desired message across the paper strips.

Inside Inspirations

Glory to God in the highest heaven, and on earth peace among those whom he favors! —Luke 2:14

O God, you make us glad by the yearly festival of the birth of your only Son Jesus Christ: Grant that we, who joyfully receive him as our Redeemer, may with sure confidence

behold him when he comes to be our Judge; who lives and reigns with you and the Holy Spirit, one God, now and for ever. Amen.—Book of Common Prayer, 212

May this blessed season bring you peace and joy.

TIP: ***If you can't find silver circle stickers, cut them from silver paper using a circle maker.***

Musical Rendition

As shown on page 40.

Recognize a favorite Christmas carol with a card that comes together harmoniously.

> Folded card size: 6 inches square
>
> Envelope size: 6$^1/_2$ inches square

Supplies

- ruler
- pencil
- scoring tool
- 6x12-inch piece of white cardstock
- music note papers in red and white
- 6x4-inch piece of Christmas paper in red, white, and green
- 8$^1/_2$ x11-inch sheet of vellum
- printer
- glue stick
- double-stick tape

Make the Card

1. Measure and mark the center of each long edge of the 6x12-inch piece of cardstock. Score the card centers using the marks as guides. Fold the paper in half along scored lines.

2. Cut a 6x4-inch piece from red music note paper. Tear along one long edge.

3. Glue the Christmas paper to the bottom half of the card. Glue the red music paper to the top half of the card, allowing the torn edge to overlap the bottom paper.

4. Tear a 6x1-inch strip from white music note paper, tearing only the long edges. Glue the strip to the card, 1/2 inch from the bottom edge of the red paper.

5. Print "Silent Night" and "Holy Night" in an appropriate font, such as 60-point Edwardian Script IT, on vellum. Tear across the tops and bottoms of the phrases, as well as to the right of Silent Night and to the left of Holy Night. Adhere the strips to the top and bottom sections of the card using double-stick tape.

Inside Inspirations

All is calm, all is bright!

O God, you have caused this holy night to shine with the brightness of the true Light: Grant that we, who have known the mystery of that Light on earth, may also enjoy him

perfectly in heaven; where with you and the Holy Spirit he lives and reigns, one God, in glory everlasting. Amen.—Book of Common Prayer, 212

Wishing you a most blessed Christmas season.

Make a joyful noise to the Lord, all the earth. Worship the Lord with gladness; come into his presence with singing.

Psalms 100:1–2

Easter Praise

As shown on page 45.

Arranged just right, springy floral papers perfectly frame glittery Easter symbols.

Folded card size: $5^1/4$ x$7^1/2$ inches

Envelope size: $5^1/2$ x$7^3/4$ inches

Supplies

ruler

pencil

scoring tool

7x$10^1/2$ -inch piece of white cardstock

7x$4^7/8$ -inch piece of embossed polka-dot paper

two $2^3/4$ -inch squares and a 1x$5^1/2$ -inch strip of floral paper

glue stick

2 coordinating dimensional Easter stickers, approximately 1x2 inches

Make the Card

1. Measure and mark the center of each long edge of the 7x$10^1/2$ -inch piece of cardstock. Score the card center using the marks as a guide. Fold the paper in half along scored line.

2. Glue the polka-dot paper to the card front, allowing a narrow border on the left side. Arrange the paper squares and strips as shown, allowing room for sticker placement. Glue papers to card front.

3. Adhere the stickers to the card front.

Easter Praise; instructions, pages 44 and 46.
On the Hunt; instructions, page 47.

O sing to the Lord a new song; sing to the Lord, all the earth. Sing to the Lord, bless his name; tell of his salvatioin from day to day.

Psalms 96:1-2

Inside Inspirations

Hallelujah! He is risen!

Rejoice and sing now, all the round earth, bright with a glorious splendor, for darkness has been vanquished by our eternal King. —Book of Common Prayer, 286

But the angel said to the women, "Do not be afraid; I know that you are looking for Jesus who was crucified. He is not here; for he has been raised, as he said. Come, see the place where he lay. Then go quickly and tell his disciples, 'He has been raised from the dead, and indeed he is going ahead of you to Galilee; there you will see him.' This is my message for you." —Matt. 28:5–7

On the Hunt

As shown on page 45.

A one-sided card with Easter eggs representing new life delivers a whimsical invitation packed with fun.

Card size: $4^1/_4$ x$5^1/_2$ inches

Envelope size: $4^3/_8$ x$5^3/_4$ inches

Supplies

fine-tip black pen

$4^1/_4$ x$5^1/_2$ -inch one-sided cards

Easter egg and/or egg-hunting stickers

Make the Card

1. Write the invitation information in lines or around the edge of the card.

2. Arrange and apply stickers to the card, centering one below lines of text, or placing several stickers in the center of the text outline.

TIP: *You can reduce the amount of handwriting on an invitation if the envelope return label states your church's name and address.*

CHAPTER THREE
EVERYDAY BLESSINGS

The Lord is good to all, and his compassion
is over all that he has made.

PSALMS 145:9

As I age, I seem to become more forgetful of some things—dates, appointments, details. But the times someone went out of their way just to tell me that I was in their thoughts. . . well, those moments are ingrained in my mind forever.

In our fast-paced world, it seems we often get caught up in our personal routines. Our obligations can overtake us until we begin to take life's blessings for granted. As Christians, we strive not to be swallowed up by schedules. We try diligently to take the time to be a good neighbor, friend, relative, and citizen.

I am blessed to have a best friend who constantly stokes my spiritual fire. She doesn't need to refer to a calendar to send me a card—no holiday or special occasion is needed. When I see her return label on an envelope, I know

OPPOSITE: *Basket of Blooms; instructions, pages 51–53.*

happy thoughts are tucked inside. These "just because" cards are like children's laughter, they simply fill my soul with smiles.

This chapter sends thinking-of-you messages loud and beautifully clear with cards anyone would love receiving. Perhaps they could be used as encouragement for a visitor to return to your church or to send a heartfelt thank you. However you choose to use them, feel good knowing your efforts will brighten someone's day simply because you took the time to remember them.

Glory in his holy name; let the hearts of those who seek the Lord rejoice.

1 CHRONICLES 16:10

Basket of Blooms

As shown on page 48.

Handpick pretty papers for a fresh bouquet delivery.

Folded card size: 5x7$^1/_4$ inches

Envelope size: 5$^1/_4$ x7$^1/_2$ inches

Supplies

ruler

pencil

scoring tool

7$^1/_4$ x10-inch piece of polka-dot paper

6$^3/_4$ x4$^1/_2$ -inch piece of solid paper

5x4-inch piece of plaid paper

scraps of paper in solids and patterns

brown paper in medium and dark shades

7x9$^3/_4$ -inch piece of liner paper

paper trimmer

tracing paper

scissors

tape

double-stick tape

1-inch-diameter flower punch

large sewing needle

copper brads

glue stick

printer paper and printer

He covers the heavens with clouds, prepares rain for the earth, makes grass grow on the hills.

PSALMS 147:8

Make the Card

1. Measure and mark the center of each long edge of the 7$\frac{1}{4}$ x10-inch piece of paper. Score the card center using the marks as a guide. Fold the paper in half along scored line.

2. Glue the plaid rectangle to the solid color rectangle, leaving equal borders on the top, bottom, and left side. In the right margin, punch out three equally spaced flowers.

3. Center and glue the orange paper to the card front.

4. Cut three 4x$\frac{1}{2}$-inch-wide strips from dark brown paper. Cut seven 2x$\frac{1}{2}$-inch-wide strips from medium brown paper. Align the dark brown strips horizontally and tape at left edge. Weave in the medium brown strips. Place tape over one entire side of the weaving. Trace the basket pattern on page 107. Cut out the pattern. Trace around the pattern on the weaving and cut out. Use double-stick tape to adhere the taped side of the basket to plaid paper, centered left to right and $\frac{1}{4}$ inch from the bottom edge.

5. Punch out 11 flower shapes from various solid and pattern papers. Overlap and arrange the flowers to look as though they are in the basket.

6. Poke the sewing needle into the center of each flower shape as a guide hole. Push a brad through each hole, securing the prongs on the back.

7. Measure and mark the center of each long edge of the 7x9$\frac{3}{4}$-inch piece of liner paper. Score the paper using the marks as a guide. Fold the paper in half along scored line and glue to the inside of the card.

8. Print off a tiny message to tuck into the bouquet, such as "thinking of you" in 26-point French Script MT font with a border. Trim around message and glue to card.

Inside Inspirations

> . . . and sending you a bouquet of good wishes.

> Praying for you.

---

*TIP: **You can embellish flowers with other crafts supplies, too. Try adhesive-backed foam circles, gems, or mini pom-poms to dot flower centers.***

Moving Messages

As shown on page 55.

Whimsical pinwheels deliver uplifting thoughts for any joyous occasion. Leave blades dimensional for hand deliveries or flatten them to send through the mail.

Folded card size: 6 inches square

Envelope size: $6^{1}/_{2}$ inches square

Supplies

ruler

pencil

scoring tool

6x12-inch piece of white cardstock

$5^{3}/_{4}$ -inch square of solid color paper

two 5-inch squares of coordinating patterned paper or one double-sided square scissors

small paper punch

paper fastener

glue stick

1$\frac{1}{2}$ -inch-diameter circle maker

vellum sentiment to fit in 1$\frac{1}{2}$ -inch-diameter circle

adhesive foam spacer

Make the Card

1. Measure and mark the center of each long edge of the 6x12-inch piece of cardstock. Score the card center using the marks as a guide. Fold the paper in half along scored line.

2. Glue the 5$\frac{3}{4}$ -inch square centered on the card front.

3. If using two 5-inch squares of paper, glue with wrong sides together. Referring to the illustration on page 108, use a ruler to draw an X on the paper, corners to corners. Use scissors to cut along the lines without cutting through the center of the square. Make holes where indicated on the illustration using a paper punch.

4. Thread the prongs of the paper fastener through the outer punched holes, folding in the blades one by one. Push the fastener through the center hole and spread apart the prongs.

5. Glue the pinwheel to the card. Press gently to flatten slightly for hand delivery; press firmly for mail delivery.

6. Cut out the vellum sentiment using the circle maker. Attach the vellum to the head of the paper fastener using an adhesive spacer.

Moving Messages; instructions, pages 53–54 and 56.

Inside Inspirations

> Love makes the world go round . . . and round . . . and round . . .
>
> Thanks! Thanks! Thanks! Thanks!

TIP: *Mail this card in a rectangular envelope to avoid surcharges associated with square envelopes. (See page 98.)*

Initial Interest

As shown on page 57.

Personalize a note card with an initial, monogram, or church name as the focal point.

> Folded card size: 4x5$^{1}/_{2}$ inches
>
> Envelope size: 4$^{3}/_{8}$ x5$^{3}/_{4}$ inches

Supplies

> ruler
>
> pencil
>
> scoring tool
>
> 4$^{1}/_{2}$ x8-inch piece of white cardstock
>
> 4 coordinating print papers cut to 2$^{1}/_{4}$ x2$^{3}/_{4}$, 2$^{1}/_{4}$ x2$^{1}/_{2}$, 1$^{1}/_{2}$ x2$^{3}/_{4}$, and 1$^{1}/_{2}$ x2$^{1}/_{2}$ inches
>
> 1$^{1}/_{4}$ -inch square of silver paper
>
> glue stick
>
> printer paper and printer

Initial Interest; instructions, pages 56 and 58.

adhesive foam spacer

eight $3/8$-inch-square mosaic stickers to coordinate with print papers, 2 dark, 4 medium, and 2 light

print paper to line envelope flap, optional

Make the Card

1. Measure and mark the center of each long edge of the $4^1/2$ x8-inch piece of paper. Score the card center using the marks as a guide. Fold the paper in half along scored line.

2. Glue the four rectangles to the card front, the taller pieces on the top.

3. Print an initial in a bold font, such as 48-point Castellar. Cut out the initial in a 1-inch diamond shape. Glue the initial to the silver paper and attach it to the card where the print papers meet using an adhesive foam spacer.

4. Press mosaic stickers on-point around the initial as shown.

5. If a lined envelope flap is desired, trace around flap on print paper. Cut out slightly smaller than tracing to allow envelope glue strip to show. Glue the paper to the flap.

TIP: *When printing initials, print several on a sheet, leaving ample space around each letter for trimming. Print each letter of the alphabet and keep in a folder to save time and paper when making more initial cards.*

TIP: *If your church is named for a saint, consider making cards with the church name on the front and an excerpt from an appropriate prayer on the inside. For example, for a church named for St. Francis, the inside message could be: "Lord, make us instruments of your peace. . .".*

TIP: *You can stack adhesive foam spacers for added height. However, keep postal regulations in mind if the card will be delivered through the mail (see page 98 regarding guidelines for mail thickness).*

Photo Graphic

As shown on page 86.

Share the welcoming beauty of your church with easy-to-make photo cards.

Folded card size: $4^1/4$ x$6^1/4$ inches

Envelope size: $4^3/4$ x$6^1/2$ inches

Supplies

ruler

pencil

scoring tool

$6^1/4$ x$8^1/2$ -inch piece of white cardstock

4x6-inch photo

vellum sentiment printed to fit photo space

double-stick tape

Make the Card

1. Measure and mark the center of each long edge of the $6^1/4$ x$8^1/2$ -inch piece of cardstock. Score the card center using the marks as guides. Fold the paper in half along scored lines.

2. Use double-stick tape to adhere the photo to the card front.

3. Decide the positioning for the vellum sentiment and secure it in place using double-stick tape.

TIP: ***Ask church members to donate multiple copies of their best church photos to use for your card ministry.***

Kid Connections

As shown on page 61.

Speak to the kids of the congregation and community with delightful sticker cards you can make in seconds.

Folded card size: 4x5 inches

Envelope size: $4^1/_8$ x$5^1/_2$ inches

Supplies

ruler

pencil

scoring tool

5x8-inch piece of watercolor-look paper

white cardstock and glue stick, optional

black fine-tip pen

stickers

Kid Connections; instructions, pages 60 and 62.

Inside Inspirations

Jesus loves you, this I know!

A child of God—how blessed you are!

Make the Card

1. Measure and mark the center of each long edge of the 5x8-inch piece of paper. Score the card center using the marks as a guide. Fold the paper in half along scored line.

2. Place a sticker in the center of the card front. If the background paper is dark, first place the sticker on white cardstock and trim a narrow border around the sticker. Use glue stick to adhere the paper-backed sticker to the card.

3. Draw a pair of squiggly rules around the edges of the card.

Quilted Expressions

As shown on page 64.

Piece together heartwarming cards by arranging paper triangles in the pattern of a cozy quilt.

Folded card size: 4$\frac{1}{2}$ inches square

Envelope size: 5 inches square

Supplies

ruler

pencil

scoring tool

4$\frac{1}{2}$ x9-inch piece of white cardstock

3 coordinating patterned papers

1$\frac{1}{2}$-inch square punch

paper trimmer

glue stick

long-reach paper punch

sewing needle

embroidery floss

scissors

Let everything that breathes praise the Lord! Praise the Lord!

Quilted Expressions; instructions, pages 63 and 65.

Make the Card

1. Measure and mark the center of each long edge of the 4$\frac{1}{2}$ x9-inch piece of cardstock. Score the card center using the marks as a guide. Fold the paper in half along scored line.

2. From the three patterned papers, punch two squares from two of the papers and four squares from the remaining paper. Use a paper trimmer to cut the squares in half from opposite points.

3. Mark the center of the card front. Arrange the paper triangles as shown to resemble a patchwork quilt. Glue the pieces to the card.

4. Use a long-reach paper punch to make a pair of holes at the five interior positions where the triangle points meet.

5. Thread the needle with embroidery floss. Starting at the right side, push the needle through one hole and bring it back through the other. Knot the floss ends and trim to $\frac{1}{2}$ inch.

Inside Inspirations

> You have made known to me the ways of life; you will make me full of gladness with your presence. Acts 2:28

> May God's teachings inhabit your soul and bless your life.

Bright and Cheery Blessings

As shown on page 67.

Send a cheerful card brimming with color, good wishes, and a surprise personalized bookmark waiting inside.

Folded card size: 4x9 inches

Envelope size: $4^{1}/_{8}$ x$9^{1}/_{2}$ inches

Bookmark size: 2x$8^{5}/_{8}$ inches

Supplies for the Card

ruler

pencil

scoring tool

9x8-inch piece of white cardstock

$8^{1}/_{4}$ x2-inch piece of orange paper

$8^{1}/_{4}$ x$^{5}/_{8}$ -inch piece of striped cardstock

paper scraps in coordinating patterns

$1^{1}/_{2}$ -inch-diameter circle punch

glue stick

vellum sentiment

Make the Card

1. Measure and mark the center of each short edge of the 9x8-inch piece of white cardstock. Score the card center using the marks as a guide. Fold the paper in half along scored line.

2. Glue the orange paper rectangle to the card front with the top and side borders even. Adhere the striped paper rectangle in place with the bottom and side borders even.

Bright and Cheery Blessings; instructions, pages 66 and 68.
Tags All Abloom; instructions, pages 69–70.

3. Cut out five circles from patterned papers. Glue evenly spaced across orange paper rectangle. Adhere vellum sentiment between paper rectangles, aligned with the right edges.

Inside Inspirations

Sending cheerful thoughts your way!

Happy day, happy reading!

Supplies for the Bookmark

2x8⁵⁄₈ -inch piece of striped cardstock

1³⁄₄ x8¹⁄₄ -inch piece of turquoise paper

paper scraps in coordinating patterns and a solid color

1¹⁄₂ -inch-diameter circle punch

glue stick

1¹⁄₄ -inch-high alphabet sticker

Make the Bookmark

1. Glue the turquoise paper rectangle to the striped cardstock, even with the top edge and centered left to right.

2. Cut out five circles from patterned and solid papers. Glue evenly spaced down turquoise paper rectangle. Press sticker letter onto one of the circles.

Tags All Abloom

As shown on page 67.

Pretty posies, backed with tag shapes, parade joyfully across a horizontal card.

Folded card size: 4x9 inches

Envelope size: $4^{1}/_{8}$ x$9^{1}/_{2}$ inches

Supplies

ruler

pencil

scoring tool

9x8-inch piece of white cardstock

$3^{1}/_{4}$ x$8^{1}/_{2}$-inch piece of turquoise paper

3x6-inch piece of multi-color floral paper

scraps of paper in purple and white

paper trimmer

tag punch, approximately $1^{3}/_{4}$ x$2^{3}/_{4}$ inches

circle punches in $1^{1}/_{4}$- and $1^{1}/_{2}$-inch diameters

3 eyelets and eyelet tool

glue stick

embroidery floss in pink and orange

2 pink and 1 orange miniature silk daisy stickers

blue fine-tip pen

Make the Card

1. Measure and mark the center of each short edge of the 9x8-inch piece of white cardstock. Score the card center using the marks as a guide. Fold the paper in half along scored line.

2. Cut a $1^1/_2$ -inch strip off the long edge of the turquoise paper. Adhere the two turquoise strips to the front of the card leaving a narrow space between the strips.

3. Use the circle punches to make four $1^1/_4$ -inch circles from white paper and four $1^1/_2$ -inch circles from purple paper. Center and glue a white circle on each purple circle. Stick a flower on three of the circles and write a message on the fourth.

4. Use the tag punch to cut three shapes from floral paper. Secure an eyelet to each tag top following the eyelet manufacturer's instructions. Cut three 4-inch-long pieces of embroidery floss, two from pink and one from red. For each tag, fold the floss piece in half, thread the loop through the eyelet, and pull the floss tails through the loop. Center a flower on each tag.

5. Arrange and glue the tags and message circle evenly spaced across the card front. Tape the floss ends to the back side of the card.

Inside Inspirations

   . . . on this, your special day.

   . . . and all our best wishes from your friends at (insert name of church).

Love One Another
As shown on page viii.

Flower shapes in a bouquet of bright colors freshen up a bold symbol of love.

   Folded card size: $5^3/_4$ x8 inches

   Envelope size: 6x$8^1/_4$ inches

Supplies

> ruler
>
> pencil
>
> scoring tool
>
> 8x11$^{1}/_{2}$ -inch piece of white cardstock
>
> 5$^{1}/_{2}$ x7$^{3}/_{4}$ -inch piece of orange paper
>
> 5$^{1}/_{2}$ x7$^{1}/_{2}$ -inch piece of red paper
>
> paper scraps in green, yellow, pink, silver, and shades of blue
>
> paper trimmer
>
> flower punch, approximately 1 inch diameter
>
> paper punch
>
> glue stick
>
> vellum sentiment

Make the Card

1. Measure and mark the center of each long edge of the 8x11$^{1}/_{2}$ -inch piece of white cardstock. Score the card center using the marks as a guide. Fold the paper in half along scored line.

2. Trace the heart pattern, page 99. Use the pattern to cut a heart from the red paper.

3. Use the flower punch to cut out shapes randomly on the right side of the heart and from paper scraps. Punch flowers and circles in the upper left and lower right corners of the orange rectangle.

4. Center and glue the heart on the orange paper rectangle; adhere to card front. Glue flower centers to the heart, using the photo as a guide.

5. Position vellum phrase diagonally on card front, tucking between petals to hold it in place. Tack in place with glue if needed.

Glory in his holy name; let the hearts of those who seek the Lord rejoice.

PSALMS 105:3

CHAPTER FOUR

JOURNEY OF FAITH

Teach me your way, O Lord, that I may walk
in your truth; give me an undivided heart
to revere your name.

PSALMS 86:11

As Christians, we may find that our religious growth is often linked to
our life experiences. For me, my belief and devotion to God has been strength-
ened in so very many ways, but particularly as I've witnessed miracles, such as
the healing of a very dear friend who had relentless cancer in her sinuses. My
faith multiplies daily as I am endlessly showered with his abundant blessings
and promise of forgiveness. As I watch my children experience those faith-
building "ah-ha" moments, I too am moved along my path.

When my son was going through confirmation last year, I thought about how
structured it was compared to when I was going through that time in my life.
These kids experienced more than just a weekly class and taking notes in church.
There was time set aside to help the less fortunate. There was a week of Bible
camp full of new, wonderful experiences. And there was Discovery Weekend.

OPPOSITE: *Baptismal Celebrations; instructions, pages 75–78.*

But grow in the grace and knowledge of our Lord and Savior Jesus Christ. To him be the glory both now and to the day of eternity. Amen.

2 PETER 3:18

In preparation for the weekend, we were asked to secretly gather uplifting letters from friends and relatives that would be given to our son during the gathering. As the cards and letters were given to me, I cried as I read each one. What a wonderful son I have. What glorious things God can do through him. What a blessing he is!

It wasn't that the words written in the cards surprised me or were even new to me. It was the affirmation of my feelings, the strength of the written words, and the compassion for my son that struck me. Those cards and letters inspired me to be more open with my words, to praise God and his servants for work well done.

The cards in this chapter honor not only confirmation, but also baptism, first communion, and holy matrimony. These sacred traditions provide opportunities to keep the lines of communication open with other Christians through gracious cards of recognition.

While young children being baptized cannot appreciate a card right away, they will when they are older and going through keepsakes from their entrance into the Christian community. A note from their church offering welcome will remind them of the love we share as Christians.

A similar feeling of belonging can be invoked by cards for those receiving first communion or being confirmed or received. We can remind children (and adults) going through these rites of passage that this is more than ceremony; it is a joyous, life-altering step into the fellowship of believers.

The same sort of support should be shown to those couples entering marriage. In most Christian denominations, the service of holy matrimony includes a call to those in attendance to do all in their power to help the couple on their journey together. A card from their church family offering congratulations and good wishes is a symbol of that support.

Baptismal Celebrations

As shown on page 72.

Honor the sacred ceremony of baptism with an artistic charm card.

Folded card size: 4³/4 x7 inches

Envelope size: 5¹/4 x7¹/2 inches

Supplies for the Vertical Card

ruler
pencil
scoring tool
7x9¹/2 -inch piece of white cardstock
5x7-inch piece of patterned paper
7x¹/4 -inch piece of metallic gold paper
2¹/4 -inch-diameter circle maker
glue stick
vellum sentiment
double-stick tape
silver cross charm
pliers
small adhesive foam spacers

Make the Card

1. Measure and mark the center of each long edge of the 7x9¹/2 -inch piece of cardstock. Score the card center using the marks as a guide. Fold the paper in half along scored line.

2. Use the circle maker to cut a circle from the right edge of the patterned paper, approximately 2 inches from the bottom. Tear away the straight edges of the paper, tearing off the right side of the cutout circle.

3. Glue the gold paper strip along the right edge of the card front. Center and glue the torn-edge paper to the card front.

4. Tear the top and bottom edges of the vellum sentiment; trim to fit card. Adhere the vellum strip overlapping the cutout circle, using double-stick tape at the ends.

5. Bend off the hanging loop of the charm with pliers. Use four small foam spacers to affix the cross in the center of the circle.

Supplies for the Horizontal Card

> ruler
> pencil
> scoring tool
> $7^{1}/_{4}$ x$8^{1}/_{2}$ -inch piece of white cardstock
> $7^{1}/_{4}$ x4-inch piece of background paper
> $4^{1}/_{2}$ x4-inch piece of subtle-pattern paper
> $7^{1}/_{4}$ x$^{1}/_{8}$ -inch piece of metallic gold paper
> $2^{1}/_{4}$ -inch-diameter circle maker
> glue stick
> vellum sentiment
> double-stick tape
> silver cross charm
> pliers
> small adhesive foam spacers

Make the Card

1. Measure and mark the center of each long edge of the 7$1/4$ x8$1/2$ -inch piece of cardstock. Score the card center using the marks as a guide. Fold the paper in half along scored line.

2. Align the background paper with the fold; glue in place. Glue the gold paper strip along the bottom edge of the background paper.

3. Use the circle maker to cut a circle from the center right edge of the subtle-pattern paper. Tear away the straight edges of the paper, tearing off the right side of the cutout circle. Glue the torn-edge paper to the card front, approximately $1/2$ inch from the left edge.

4. Tear the top and bottom edges of the vellum sentiment; trim to fit card. Adhere the vellum strip overlapping the cutout circle, using double-stick tape at the ends.

5. Bend off the hanging loop of the charm with pliers. Use four small foam spacers to affix the cross in the center of the circle.

Inside Inspirations

As many of you as were baptized into Christ have clothed yourselves with Christ. —Gal. 3:27

Touched by water. Saved by Christ. Loved by God. What a glorious day to celebrate with you.

There is one Body and one Spirit;
There is one hope in God's call to us;
One Lord, one Faith, one Baptism;
One God and Father of all.
—Book of Common Prayer, 299

For just as the body is one and has many members, and all the members of the body, though many, are one body, so it is with Christ.

1 Corinthians 12:12

TIP: *Incorporate a gift into the card by using a cross necklace for the embellishment. Remove the chain and place it in an envelope taped to the back of the card.*

First Communion Wishes

As shown on page 79.

A beautiful card, embellished with gilded touches, glorifies the unforgettable day of a First Holy Communion.

Folded card size: 6 inches square

Envelope size: 6^1/$_2$ inches square

Supplies

ruler

pencil

scoring tool

6x12-inch piece of cream and metallic gold cardstock

4^1/$_2$ x7-inch piece of purple and metallic gold paper

8^1/$_2$ x11-inch piece of cream paper

printer

glue stick

dimensional dove embellishment

adhesive foam spacers

First Communion Wishes; instructions, pages 78 and 80.

Make the Card

1. Measure and mark the center of each long edge of the 6x12-inch piece of cardstock. Score the card center using the marks as guides. Fold the cardstock in half along scored lines.

2. Glue the purple and metallic gold paper strip centered on the card front, wrapping the extra inch to the back side of the card.

3. Keeping within a 5¹/₂ x5-inch space, type Matthew 26:26–28 using an appropriate font, such as 24-point Vivaldi, in purple, allowing space for the dove embellishment on the right side. Type "First Communion Blessings" below the passage using a complementary font, such as 24-point Georgia, in blue. Print out the message on cream paper and trim to 5¹/₂ x5 inches. Glue to the center of the card front.

4. Use adhesive foam spacers to attach the dove embellishment to the card.

Inside Inspirations

What a blessed day!

How wonderful to witness your First Communion. Our love and prayers are yours today and always.

Spirit Alive

As shown on page 82.

Get kids involved in making these torn-paper creations that are bursting with color and faith.

> Folded card size: 5 inches square
>
> Envelope size: 5¹/₂ inches square

Supplies

> ruler
>
> pencil
>
> scoring tool
>
> 5x10-inch piece of blue or peach cardstock
>
> Cardstock in shades of blue and purple or pink and shades of orange
>
> glue stick
>
> Jesus car emblem or confirmation token
>
> adhesive foam spacers

Make the Card

1. Measure and mark the center of each long edge of the 5x10-inch piece of cardstock. Score the card center using the marks as guides. Fold the paper in half along scored lines.

2. To make the cross card, tear strips of varying widths from the pieces of blue and purple cardstock. Use the brightest paper color to tear two strips to symbolize the cross. Adhere the torn papers to the card front, trimming the edges even. Stick the Jesus emblem to the center of the cross.

O give thanks to the God of heaven, for his steadfast love endures forever.

Psalms 136:26

Spirit Alive; instructions, pages 81 and 83.

3. To make the sunburst card, tear long wedges from the pieces of pink and orange cardstock. Arrange them to appear as sun rays. Adhere the torn papers to the card front, trimming the edges even. Affix the token to the tips of the rays using adhesive foam spacers.

Inside Inspirations

> Showered in love forever. Amen!
>
> Strengthen, O Lord, your servant (name) with your Holy Spirit; empower him/her for your service; and sustain him/her all the days of his/her life. Amen.—Book of Common Prayer, 418
>
> Blessings to you on this very special day of confirmation.

Simply Love

As shown on page 85.

With a window-style photo card and a one-color stamped image, you can make a stunning card for the bride and groom in minutes.

> Folded card size: $4^1/4$ x$5^1/2$ inches
>
> Envelope size: $4^3/8$ x$5^3/4$ inches

Supplies

> window-style photo card
> cardstock in desired color
> white cardstock
> stamp in wedding or floral motif to fit in window space on card
> stamp pad in black or metallic gold
> paper trimmer

> double-stick tape
> black fine-tip pen
> adhesive acrylic gems

Make the Card

1. Cut a piece of colored cardstock slightly larger than the card window. Slip it into the card and secure with double-stick tape.

2. Stamp a wedding image on white cardstock; let dry. Trim around the stamped image, allowing a narrow border of the background color to show. Tape the stamped image in the center of the window. Embellish the stamped motif with adhesive acrylic gems.

3. Write "holy matrimony" below the window opening.

Inside Inspirations

Therefore a man leaves his father and mother and clings to his wife, and they become one flesh. —Gen. 2:24

And now faith, hope, and love abide, these three; and the greatest of these is love. —1 Cor. 13:13

Let their love for each other be a seal upon their hearts, a mantle about their shoulders, and a crown upon their foreheads. —Book of Common Prayer, 430

TIP: *You can create your own window cards by measuring and marking the desired opening. Cut out the window using a metal ruler and a crafts knife.*

Simply Love; instructions, pages 83–84.

For where two or three are gathered in my name, I am there among them.

Matthew

faith love hope

CHAPTER FIVE

ORGANIZING A CARD MINISTRY TEAM

Like good stewards of the manifold grace
of God, serve one another with
whatever gift each of you has received.

—1 PETER 4:10

A card ministry team can be vital to the communication system within a church, a community, and beyond. Each member of the group is truly a missionary, reaching out to people in all phases of life, sharing God's love.

Gather a Team

Ask for volunteers who feel the calling to serve as a wordsmith for God. No real skills or experience are needed, simply a willingness to be a link in the

OPPOSITE: *Photo Graphic; instructions, pages 59–60.*

communication chain. Depending on the circumstances, such as the number of volunteers and the size of the church, people on the Card Ministry Team can embrace a single task or choose multiple responsibilities.

This can be a truly multi-generational ministry. Children can help with making cards or stamping envelopes, and while their products may not be of the same standard as those of the adult members of the team, few people will fail to be charmed when they receive a personal, handmade card from a child. At the other end of the age spectrum, the seniors in the church are a valuable resource for their life experience and knowledge of the parish's past. If someone is prevented from working on card construction by an infirmity such as failing eyesight or arthritis, he or she can take on other important duties, as outlined below.

Decide Roles

While making and sending cards to an entire congregation may seem overwhelming, it's quite doable when broken up into can-do jobs.

- Information Gatherer—the person who is notified by church staff when events take place in the life of the church members, such as births, weddings, hospitalizations, illnesses, deaths, milestone anniversaries, etc. This person is in charge of setting up a system to inform the Card Ministry Team about such occasions. Reoccurring occasions, such as birthdays or keeping in touch with shut-ins, should be itemized in a calendar format. Information relayed to the card ministry team may come by way of phone calls, personal communication, prayer cards, card request boxes, and notes on pew memo pads. The team should also scan newspapers for awards and other newsworthy items that deserve to be honored. As the team moves forward to satisfy the church's communication needs, keep in mind that some matters that are brought to your attention may be confidential and do not warrant cards, but silent prayers.

• Supply Coordinator—the person who makes sure the Card Ministry Team has sufficient card-making materials, envelopes, church return address labels, and stamps on hand. (See the individual projects for detailed supply lists as well as the suggested Basic Card Making Supply Kit on page 97). A good cost-cutting idea is to ask members of the church to donate old greeting cards. The cards can be cut apart to use the decorative parts of the paper and the inside messages can be recycled. Along with the responsibility of the coordinator comes that of a treasurer, arranging for funding and supply donations.

• Card Maker—the person who crafts the cards. If desired, cards can be made assembly-line fashion, if several people offer to pitch in.

• Writer—the person, preferably with neat penmanship, who personalizes the inside messages and signs the cards on behalf of the team or church. Or, encourage church members to add their signatures by placing the cards in a designated area of the church.

• Mail Deliverer—the person who makes sure the envelopes are properly sealed, addressed, stamped, and mailed or delivered in person.

Start with a Prayer

As the card ministry team gathers together, take time to bow heads and share in a moment of prayer, asking God's blessing upon your purpose.

> Dear Heavenly Father, please guide us as we join together to reach out to others in the loving spirit You have taught us. Open our minds and hearts to the needs of others. Let us be creative in our efforts. Grant us the wisdom to choose the right words so that the recipients of these cards will know they are not alone, but are loved and treasured as one of your children. In your name we pray. Amen.

Be Aware of Needs

A helpful way many churches gather information for the card ministry team is to put a card request box equipped with information-gathering slips in an easily accessible location in the church, such as the narthex. It would be the responsibility of the Information Gatherer to empty the box on a regular basis.

A sign posted by the box would ensure the timeliness of the communications. It should state:

Card Request Box

Please notify the Card Ministry Team two weeks ahead of occasions when a card is desired by completing a Card Request slip and placing it in the box. For urgent and unexpected needs, please call (insert Information Gatherer's Name here) at (insert phone number here).

The slips that accompany the box should read:

> Card Request
>
> Your Name: _____
>
> Your Phone Number:_____
>
> Person You Are Requesting a Card for: _____
>
> Address: _____
>
> City: _____State: _____Zip: _____
>
> Are they a member of our church?   Yes   No
>
> Reason for card:_____
>
> Do you have their permission to communicate this occasion or
>
> situation with us?_____

If your Information Gatherer has an e-mail address, you can also encourage people to make card requests that way. Listing the address on the church's website will allow people to contact him or her easily. If you Information Gatherer would rather not have his or her e-mail address posted on the website, consider creating an e-mail account specifically for this purpose through one of the free web-based e-mail services such as Yahoo!™ or Gmail.™ You may even be able to get a fitting address, such as "saint_paul_card_ministry@something.com."

Look for Opportunities

Aside from the birthdays, anniversaries, illnesses, and other events in the lives of the church members, there will be other occasions that warrant a card. Try to be aware of the community outside your church. Perhaps the couple across the street just celebrated their fiftieth wedding anniversary, or a new family has moved into the neighborhood. Members of the Card Ministry Team should try to keep in touch with the nearby community, so that these milestones can be acknowledged. If some of your parishioners live near the church, ask them to let your Information Gatherer know about such things as they hear of them.

Another opportunity for card ministry is in recognizing the efforts of those who keep the church going. Perhaps once a month the Card Ministry Team could choose someone to thank for the work they do. The priest or minister, church secretary, organist, choir director, and sexton or custodian would all appreciate notes of gratitude on behalf of the church. Depending on your particular church structure, you may want to include the Sunday school teachers, treasurer, sacristan, vestry members. . . try making a list of those who work for the church, as employees or volunteers, and you will find many people deserving of recognition.

Consider Inside Inspirations

What is written inside the card is a very important component of the greeting card. This message can be handwritten, printed from a computer, stamped with ink, recycled, or purchased where scrapbooking and card-making supplies are sold. Whatever method you use, choose the words with great care. The themed cards in this book are accompanied by "Inside Inspirations" as samples to inspire your words. Tweak the samples or develop new verses if needed to be more fitting of a situation.

Consider the age of the person receiving the message to make sure the words are age appropriate. If you are not sure of the general age of a person, try to find out. The message becomes less personal if a child receives an adult-style card and is just as true for the opposite. If you have a large congregation or get regular requests for non-members, you may not personally know many of the card recipients. If this is the case, you may want to add the following to the Card Request Slip:

This person is a: _____ Child   _____ Teenager   _____ Adult
                      _____ Male   _____ Female

Prayerfully think about the tone of the card. Is the greeting card meant to share happiness, sympathy, support, thanks, or some other message? Knowing why the card is being sent enables you to speak to the recipient in meaningful and considerate written words.

Using Bible passages is a wonderful way to share God's love and understanding. Include a Bible reference so that the recipient not only knows where the words are from, but to guide them to that part of the Bible should they wish to read more. Poetry, quotations, and messages you create yourself are other ways you can reach out in words. Ask for God's guidance in making the message inside the card as powerful as possible.

Remember Your Purpose

Staying in touch with fellow parishioners, celebrating their special times and offering support during their trials, helps to bond the members of the church to one another. Without a way to connect, it is possible for a church to be merely a group of people sharing Sunday services and then going their separate ways. While it is hoped that the members of a parish are important in one another's lives, that kind of relationship doesn't happen automatically. Church members must make an effort to strengthen the ties between them.

Likewise, outreach to the larger community is essential to the mission of the church. There are churches that exist separate from their own neighborhoods, islands of Christians closed off from the people outside the church doors. This is not what God intended, and it is not good for the long-term health of the church. We are called to be a beacon to the world, announcing and celebrating the love of Christ. A card ministry can, in its own quiet way, be one of the threads that draw us closer to one another, and thereby to God.

Waste Not, Want Not

Share your supply needs with fellow church members and businesses in the community. Their contributions will not only help you maintain a budget, but the cardmaking supplies you receive may also inspire even more greeting card designs.

Here are some items to include on your wish list:

Acrylic gems	Blank notecards and post cards
Address labels	Cake candles
Adhesive letters	Cardboard
Beads	Charms

Chenille stems

Confetti

Craft paints

Craft glue

Craft sticks

Crayons

Double-stick tape

Embroidery floss

Envelopes

Fabrics

Felts

Glitter

Glue sticks

Greeting cards

Hot-glue gun and glue sticks

Ink pads

Jute

Label makers and tape

Lace

Marking pens

Mini Bibles

Paintbrushes

Papers

Paper cutters

Paper doilies

Paper punches

Patterns

Pencils

Pens

Poetry

Postage stamps

Ribbon

Rulers

Scissors, decorative- and straight-edge

Scoring tool

Sequins

Sewing needles

Sewing thread

Shape makers

Silk flowers

Stamps

Stickers

Storage containers

String

Tags

Tape

Tissue paper

Used greeting cards

Wrapping paper

CARD-MAKING TIPS AND PATTERNS

*F*rom gathering supplies to dropping the cards in the mail, this section will guide you through all the basics.

Basic Card-Making Kit

While the papers and embellishments will change from card to card, you will use many of the same tools and supplies over and over again. Here's a list of basics to keep handy:

address list or church directory (A pictorial directory is helpful for identifying card recipients, but you should also have the most up-to-date addresses available.)

adhesive foam spacers

colored pencils

double-stick tape

envelopes in a variety of sizes

glue sticks

Mailbox Ministry book

paper trimmer

pencils

pens in several colors

return address labels

rulers

scissors

scoring tool

stamps

Post-Office Ready

To make sure your postage rates are as low as possible, be aware of the post office requirements.

Dimension Guidelines

	Minimum	Maximum
Height	$3^1/_2$ inches	$6^1/_8$ inches
Length	5 inches	$11^1/_2$ inches
Thickness	0.007 inch	$^1/_2$ inch

Any item smaller than the minimum dimensions is not mailable.

A first-class card under one ounce that meets the dimension guidelines can be mailed at the current first-class rate. Check with your post office for the additional postage required if your card and envelope weigh more than one ounce.

Surcharges will apply if an envelope is square (a 5-inch square is minimum), too rigid, addressed parallel to the shorter envelope dimension, includes strings, buttons or similar closures, or contains items making the surface uneven.

Each of the cards in this book includes the folded dimension of the card along with a suggested common envelope size. Or, if you like, you can make your own envelopes using a medium-weight paper.

Full-Size Patterns

heart pattern

LOVE ONE ANOTHER

Instructions appear on page 70.
Photo appears on page viii.

SANCTUARY SYMBOLS

Instructions appear on pages 7 and 9.

Photo appears on page 8.

cross pattern, inside

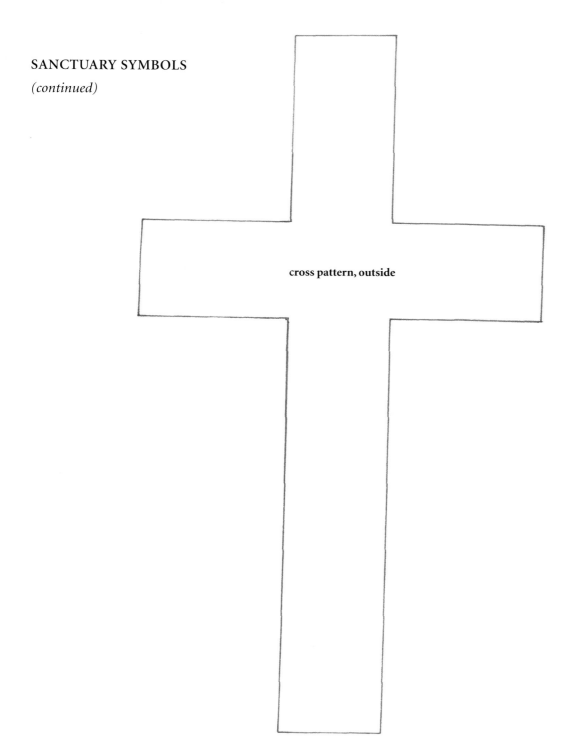

cross pattern, outside

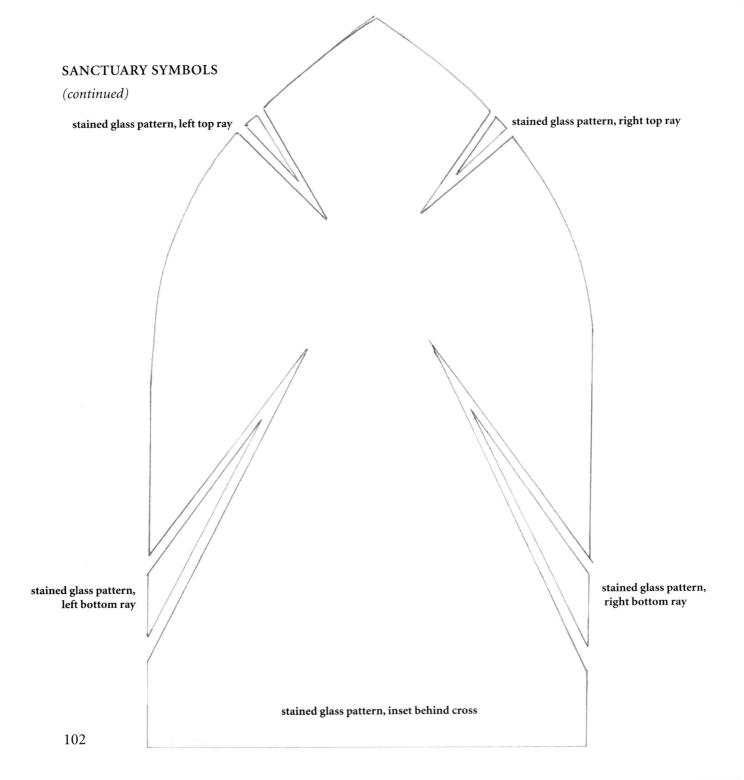

SANCTUARY SYMBOLS

(continued)

stained glass pattern, left top ray

stained glass pattern, right top ray

stained glass pattern,
left bottom ray

stained glass pattern,
right bottom ray

stained glass pattern, inset behind cross

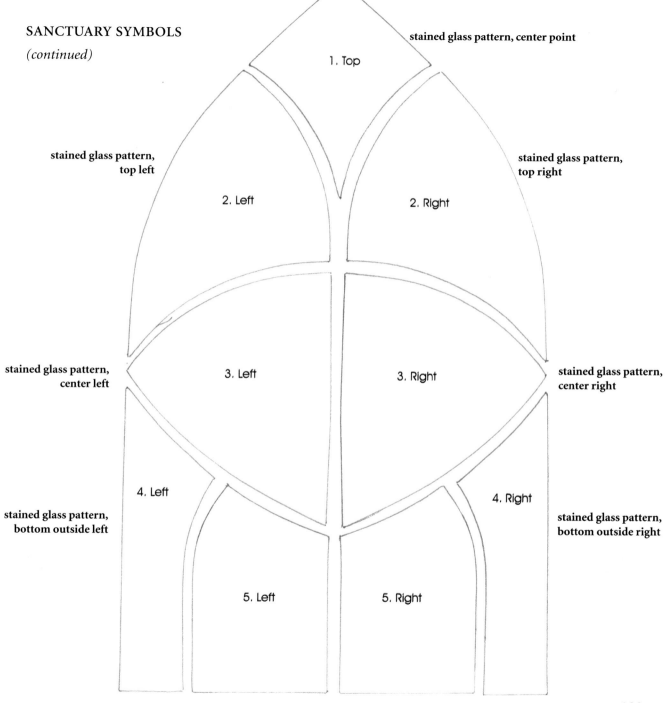

SANCTUARY SYMBOLS

(continued)

stained glass pattern, center point

1. Top

stained glass pattern,
top left

stained glass pattern,
top right

2. Left

2. Right

stained glass pattern,
center left

stained glass pattern,
center right

3. Left

3. Right

4. Left

4. Right

stained glass pattern,
bottom outside left

stained glass pattern,
bottom outside right

5. Left

5. Right

stained glass pattern, bottom inside left

stained glass pattern, bottom inside right

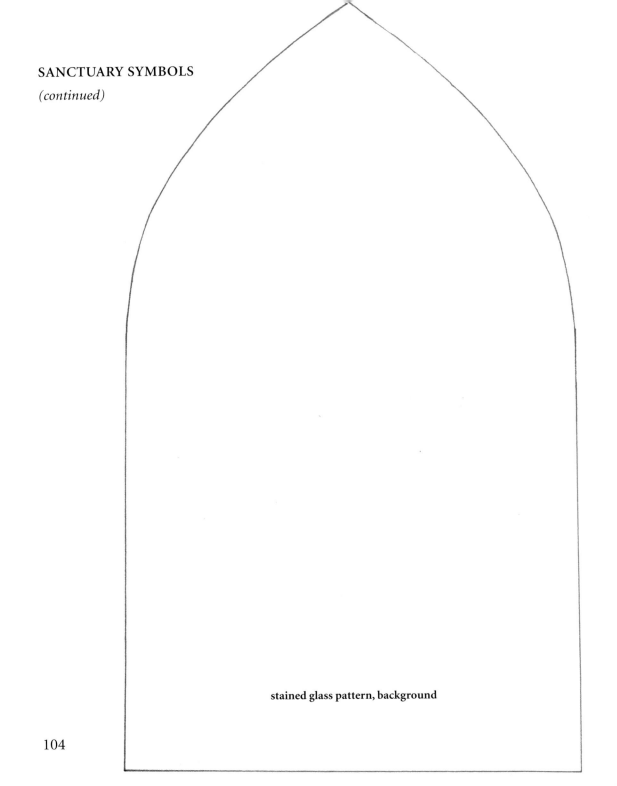

stained glass pattern, background

THOUGHTFUL STITCHES

Instructions appear on page 19.
Photo appears on page 20.

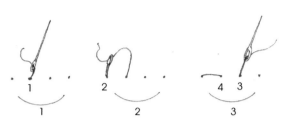

stitching diagram

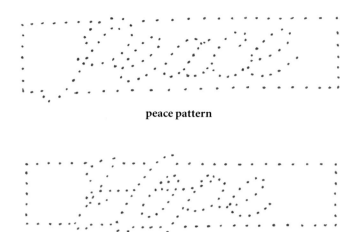

peace pattern

hope pattern

WEE-ONE WELCOME

Instructions appear on page 27.
Photo appears on page 22.

T-shirt pattern

SWEET THOUGHTS

Instructions appear on page 34.
Photo appears on page 33.

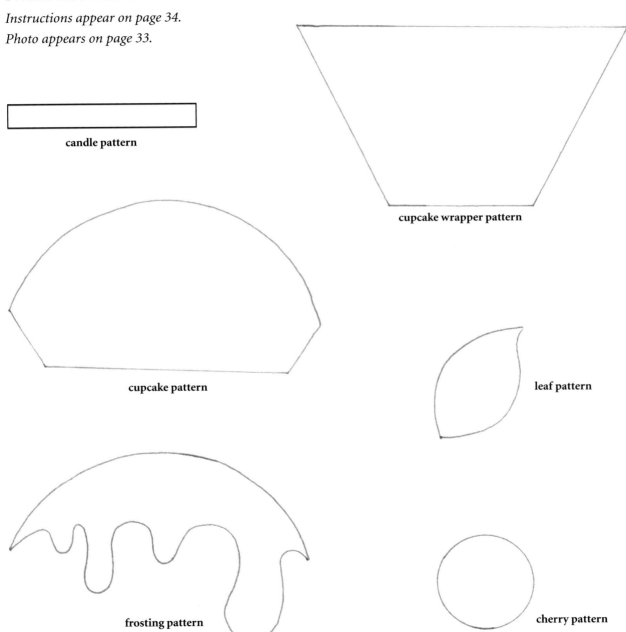

candle pattern

cupcake wrapper pattern

cupcake pattern

leaf pattern

frosting pattern

cherry pattern

DAINTY DOLIES

Instructions appear on page 35.
Photo appears on page 37.

heart pattern

BASKET OF BLOOMS

Instructions appear on page 51.
Photo appears on page 48.

basket pattern

MOVING MESSAGES

Instructions appear on page 53.

Photo appears on page 55.

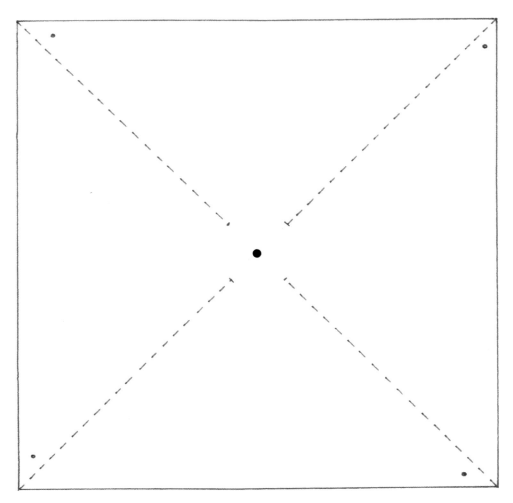

pinwheel cutting diagram

GLOSSARY

Adhesive foam spacer—An adhesive foam spacer is a 3-D piece of foam that has adhesive on both sides. Available in a variety of sizes, these adhesive risers lift small embellishments from the card surface. Adhesive foam spacers can be purchased in crafts, discount, and scrapbook stores.

Brads—Brads, or paper fasteners, have two prongs that insert through the surface of the paper, separate, and press flat to secure. These decorative embellishments come in a variety of styles and colors. Brads are available at art, crafts, discount, office supply, and scrapbook stores.

Cardstock—A thick, sturdy paper that is available in a variety of weights and colors. Cardstock can be purchased in art, crafts, discount, and scrapbook stores.

Crafts glue—A white glue that dries clear. Use it for bonding heavyweight papers or non-metal crafts embellishments. Avoid using crafts glue with lightweight paper as it may cause the paper to wrinkle. Crafts glue can be purchased in crafts and discount stores.

Crafts knife—A tool with a small angled blade that fits into a pencil-size handle. Crafts knives are available at art, crafts, discount, hardware, and scrapbook stores.

Crop—To crop means to cut away an unwanted area of paper, such as on a photograph or decorative paper.

Decorative-edge scissors—Scissors with special blades that cut patterns, such as zigzags and scallops, into paper. Decorative-edge scissors can be purchased in crafts, discount, and scrapbook stores.

Double-stick tape—Dispensed on a roll, this tape is adhesive on both sides. Double-stick tape can be purchased in art, crafts, discount, hardware, office supply, and scrapbook stores.

Embossed paper—A paper that has designs or patterns raised from the surface. Embossed papers are available at art, crafts, and scrapbook stores.

Eyelets—Eyelets are metal rings that reinforce a hole in paper. They are made in a variety of colors, sizes, and finishes. Eyelets can be purchased in crafts, fabric, and scrapbook stores.

Eyelet tool—Eyelet tools come in two types. One is similar to a paper punch that when squeezed secures the eyelet in place. The other is a special metal rod with a pointed tip that is struck with a hammer. Eyelet tools can be purchased in crafts, fabric, and scrapbook stores.

Glue stick—A stick-style solid adhesive available in temporary and permanent bonds. The glue in some sticks is colored when applied and turns clear when dry. Glue sticks can be purchased in art, crafts, discount, and scrapbook stores.

Liner paper—Paper used to line a card to make it sturdier. Liners are used most commonly when the outer paper is lightweight instead of cardstock. Liner paper can be purchased in art, crafts, discount, and scrapbook stores.

Long-reach paper punch—A long-reach paper punch is one that can reach further from a paper edge than a typical paper punch. These punches may make a single hole, a pair of buttonholes, a pair of short dashes, or another design. Long-reach paper punches are available in crafts and scrapbook stores.

Miter—When referring to paper strips, cut the end pieces at 45-degree angles to form a corner when put together.

Paper cutter—A paper cutter is a hand-operated device with a ruler and a large blade for making straight cuts in paper. Paper cutters are available in art, crafts, discount, office supply, and scrapbook stores.

Paper punch—A paper punch is a tool that when the handles are squeezed together cuts a small shape into paper, such as circles, hearts, and stars. Paper punches are available in art, crafts, discount, office supply, and scrapbook stores.

Paper trimmer—A paper trimmer is a hand-operated device with a ruler and a small blade for making straight cuts in paper. These trimmers work best for papers that are 12 inches square or smaller. Paper trimmers are available in art, crafts, discount, office supply, and scrapbook stores.

Pinking shears—Often used for sewing, pinking shears are scissors with blades that cut in a zigzag design. Pinking shears are available in crafts, discount, fabric, and scrapbook stores.

Score—A score is a crease pressed into the surface of paper to allow it to fold accurately.

Scoring tool—A scoring tool is a blunt metal object that is dragged along a ruler to provide a straight crease. Scoring tools are available in crafts and scrapbook stores.

Scrapbook paper—Typically sold in $8^{1}/_{2}$ x11-inch sheets or 12-inch squares, scrapbook papers include solid, printed, embossed, textured, and specialty papers. Scrapbook paper can be purchased in crafts, discount, and scrapbook stores.

Spray mount— Spray mount is an aerosol-style adhesive available in temporary and permanent bonds, and should be used in a well-ventilated area. Spray mount can be purchased in art, crafts, discount, and scrapbook stores.

Tracing paper—A transparent sheet, tracing paper is placed on top of a pattern so it can be replicated. Tracing paper can be purchased in art, crafts, discount, and scrapbook stores.

Vellum—Vellum is a translucent paper that can be somewhat clear or almost opaque. It comes in a variety of colors. Vellum can be purchased in art, crafts, discount, and scrapbook stores.

INDEX